W9-BJK-479

Look for other

titles:
World's Weirdest Critters
Creepy Stuff
Odd-inary People
Amazing Escapes

Ripley's Believe It or Not!
Bizarre Bugs

by Mary Packard

and the Editors of Ripley Entertainment Inc.

illustrations by Leanne Franson

SCHOLASTIC INC.

New York   Toronto   London   Auckland   Sydney
Mexico City   New Delhi   Hong Kong   Buenos Aires

Developed by Nancy Hall, Inc.
Designed by R studio T
Cover design by Atif Toor
Photo research by Laura Miller

If you purchased this book without a cover, you should be aware that this
book is stolen property. It was reported as "unsold and destroyed" to the
publisher, and neither the author nor the publisher has received any
payment for this "stripped book."

Copyright © 2002 by Ripley Entertainment Inc.
All rights reserved. Ripley's Believe It or Not!, Believe It or Not!, and
Believe It! are registered trademarks of Ripley Entertainment Inc.
Published by Scholastic Inc. SCHOLASTIC and associated logos are
trademarks and/or registered trademarks of Scholastic Inc.

No part of this work may be reproduced, stored in a retrieval system, or
transmitted in any form or by any means, electronic, mechanical,
photocopying, recording, or otherwise, without written permission of the
publisher. For information regarding permission, write to Scholastic Inc.,
Attention: Permissions Department, 557 Broadway, New York, NY 10012.

ISBN 0-439-41768-6

12 11 10 9 8 7 6 5 4 3 2 1   2 3 4 5 6 7/0

Printed in the U.S.A.
First Scholastic printing, September 2002

Contents

Bizarre Bugs

The Ripley Experience

Robert Ripley started his career as a sports cartoonist for the *New York Globe* newspaper. One day he was having a hard time thinking of a cartoon to draw and his deadline was fast approaching. Suddenly a great idea popped into his head. Ripley dug into his files of unusual sports achievements, then quickly sketched nine of the more interesting and unusual items— and the first Believe It or Not! cartoon was born.

The cartoon was such a hit that Ripley's editor asked him to do more. Hoping that people would enjoy reading about other bizarre topics, Ripley expanded his column. Soon he was searching the globe for the weirdest things he could find. And what could be more bizarre than bugs?

Since bug behavior is among the strangest on Earth, Ripley had a steady supply of bug facts to showcase in his cartoons. Take the bombardier beetle, which sets off foul-smelling stink bombs from its backside, sending its enemies running for cover. Or the potter ant, which spends hours and hours fashioning small mud pots, one for each of her eggs. And there's the wasp that paralyzes a tarantula and buries it with one of her eggs so her soon-to-be hatched baby will have plenty of fresh food to eat. The list is endless.

Even the most common bugs are extraordinary. Everyone knows that caterpillars turn into butterflies or moths. But did you know that the young, or *nymph,* of the dragonfly lives underwater and is so fierce it can capture and eat small fish? Or that a tiny flea can jump as high as a foot—about 150 times its own body length?

Ripley was also fascinated by success stories, and bugs

are the most successful creatures on Earth. More than a million species of insects have been identified, and new ones are being discovered all the time. Making up more than five sixths of all living creatures, bugs are found everywhere, from deserts to rain forests, from hot springs to glaciers. And consider this: humans have never once been able to wipe out a single species of bug. Think of the cockroach. It was here before the dinosaurs—and it's still around today!

When asked where he got his facts, Ripley always replied, "Everywhere, and all the time. It's impossible to run dry on astonishing facts about our world." How many astonishing facts do you know about bugs? Find out by taking the Jeepers Creepers! quizzes and the Ripley's Brain Buster in each chapter. Then try the Pop Quiz at the end of the book and use the scorecard to figure out your Ripley's rank.

Welcome to the truly amazing world of bugs. It will be your strangest adventure yet.

Believe It!®

What's so bizarre about bugs? A better question might be: "What *isn't*?"

Body Count: The best way to figure out if a bug is an insect is to count its body sections. Insects' bodies are divided into three main parts: head, thorax, and abdomen. Centipedes and millipedes have lots of body sections, and spiders have just two. You can also count legs. Insects have six legs, spiders have eight, centipedes can have nearly 200 legs, and worms have no legs at all.

Jeepers Creepers!

Scientists say that for every human on Earth there are . . .

a. one million insects.
b. 200 million insects.
c. 500,000 insects.
d. 100,000 insects.

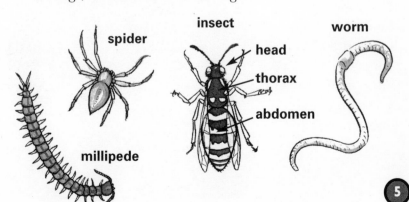

spider

insect
head
thorax
abdomen

worm

millipede

bedbug

The Skinny on Bugs:

If you want to get really technical, the only true bugs are those insects with beaklike mouthparts that can pierce and suck. Bedbugs, stinkbugs, aphids, treehoppers, and pond striders are among the true bugs.

From the Inside Out: Instead of bones, insects, spiders, centipedes, and millipedes have a hard outer covering called an *exoskeleton*. As a bug eats and gets bigger, it outgrows its exoskeleton. In this process, called *molting,* the exoskeleton splits down the middle like a pair of pants that are too tight. The bug then wriggles out (like the cicada at right is doing). It usually hides until its soft new exoskeleton hardens. Most bugs molt several times before they reach their full adult size and shape.

All Eyes Ahead: Adult insects have compound eyes that are made up of many individual eyes. Each little eye has six sides that fit with the others like a jigsaw puzzle. Having so many eyes allows an insect to detect movement from many directions at once. Though each eyelet sees

things separately, the insect's brain combines all the signals it receives to produce a complete image. Each one of a green darner dragonfly's compound eyes contains 28,000 eyelets—the most of any insect.

Seeing the Light:

Besides compound eyes, insects have another type of eye called the *ocellus*. This simple eye senses light but does not see images. Most adult insects have three ocelli, arranged in a triangle on the top of their head. The ocelli stimulate the

Jeepers Creepers!

One of the ways a cabbage white butterfly signals that she is looking for a mate is by covering her eye with . . .

a. her eyelashes.
b. a black lens.
c. an eyelid.
d. a wing.

insect to be more or less active depending on how much light there is. The brighter the light, the faster an insect will walk or fly. A housefly with its ocelli covered won't move at all.

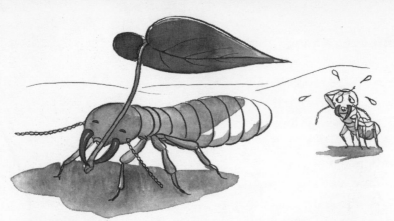

Sun Block: Termites do not like strong light. A few species carry little umbrellas made from leaves when they first come up out of the ground.

Double Vision: The whirligig beetle's compound eyes are each divided into two separate parts so it can see both above and below the water as it spins around on the surface.

Jeepers Creepers!

The color of insect blood is . . .

a. deep purple or pink.
b. royal blue.
c. milky white.
d. clear or pale yellow or green.

The Better to Hear With: Some insects, such as the brush cricket, have ears on their legs.

Belly-Full: Locusts and some grasshoppers have ears on their abdomen.

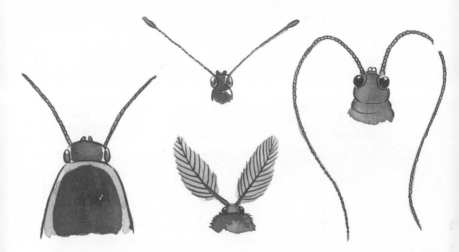

Bug Sense: One way insects make sense of their world is through their antennae, which extend from a bug's head like wires. Though antennae are used mainly for smell and touch, some insects also use them to hear and taste.

Blood Drive:

A mosquito's antennae are very sensitive to heat. That's why mosquitoes are so good at locating warm-blooded victims to feast on, even in the dark.

Ant Scents: Ants produce chemicals that have distinctive odors. They can only tell each other apart by using their antennae to touch and smell each other.

Spider Sense: In place of antennae, spiders have *pedipalps.* Located on both sides of the head, pedipalps help spiders hear, feel, taste, and touch. Most web-making spiders have poor eyesight and are only able to tell when they have trapped an insect by the vibrations they feel through their palps. Pedipalps also make great little utensils for grabbing and holding prey during dinner.

Jeepers Creepers!

Which statement is true?

a. In some parts of Africa, children tie strings to goliath beetles and keep them as pets.
b. Using their powerful back legs, goliath beetles kick stones at predators.
c. Goliath beetles have the largest wingspan of any insect.
d. A goliath beetle will travel hundreds of miles to escape a dry spell.

Putting Out Feelers:

The antennae of the long-horned beetle can be as much as three times the length of its entire body.

Lightweight Champ: At about one-tenth of a millimeter long, the wingless male firefly wasp holds the record for smallest adult insect.

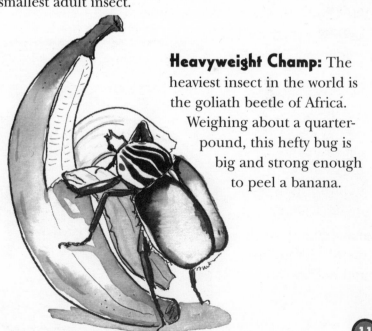

Heavyweight Champ: The heaviest insect in the world is the goliath beetle of Africa. Weighing about a quarter-pound, this hefty bug is big and strong enough to peel a banana.

Super Fly: Unlike most winged insects, the fly has only one pair of wings. In place of a second pair, it has two small knoblike structures that help keep it steady while in flight. But that doesn't stop flies from being the show-offs of the insect world. An appetizing-looking gnat on the ceiling can inspire a fly to flip itself over in midair and land upside down. The sticky pads on its feet are what make it possible for the fly to walk around while it's up there.

On the Wing:

The long "tail" at the end of each back wing gives the swallowtail butterfly its name. Its large wingspan makes it a fast and powerful flier.

Speed Dragons: One of the fastest fliers in the insect world, the dragonfly can reach speeds of over 30 miles per hour. Like most insects, it has two pairs of wings—one in front and one in back—that beat in opposite directions. As the front wings go up, the back wings go down.

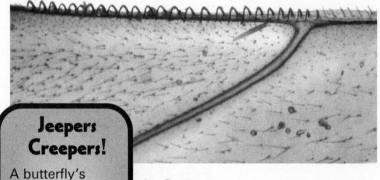

Jeepers Creepers!

A butterfly's wings are made up of . . .

a. scales that reflect light.
b. pigmented skin.
c. multicolored cells.
d. very fine hair.

In Sync: Like dragonflies, bees have two pairs of wings. But unlike the wings of the dragonfly, the bee's are connected by tiny hooks. These hooks guarantee that both sets of wings will beat together in the same direction when the bee flies.

Going the Distance: Once the weather turns cold, the monarch butterflies of North America can no longer fly. That's why they head south in the winter, flying thousands of miles to find warmth. In fact, some butterflies travel all the way from Canada to Mexico. Scientists are not entirely sure how such tiny animals are able to fly such long distances. One reason may be that their bodies are quite small compared to their wings. Another may be that the butterflies conserve energy by coasting on currents of air. But perhaps the biggest mystery is how so many butterflies end up in the very same tree that they roosted in the year before!

Do-It-Yourself Surgery: The Australian cockroach doesn't need wings because it lives underground. When it reaches maturity, it bites off its own wings.

Jeepers Creepers!

The fire beetle of Australia . . .

a. can walk through red-hot ashes.

b. gets its name from its bright scarlet coloring.

c. is used as a fire alarm because it buzzes loudly as soon as it smells smoke.

d. can start a fire by very quickly rubbing its back legs together.

Heat Seekers:

Like other insects, butterflies are cold-blooded and must get their energy to fly from solar heat. So when you see a butterfly resting on a leaf, its wings spread, soaking up the sun, it's actually warming up for the next flight.

Buzzing Off:

Mosquitoes, like other true flies, have only two wings. That annoying buzzing sound you hear when a mosquito circles your head is made by the extremely fast flapping of its wings—up to 600 times per second!

Hardly Flying:

Beetles such as ladybugs have hard front wings called *elytra*. The more delicate

back wings are hidden underneath until the beetle is ready to fly. Then it opens its front wings and flaps its back wings. The extended front wings don't flap, but help the beetle rise up into the air.

Loopy Walks:

Some caterpillars have a funky way of moving. They grasp the ground tightly with their front legs and drag their back legs forward, scrunching up their middle in a loop. To straighten out, they reach forward with their front legs, leaving their back legs in place. Then they dig in and start all over again.

Wriggling Along: Worms are a farmer's friends. As they wriggle and squirm, tunneling from place to place underground, they break up and loosen the soil so that air can circulate. The mucous on their skin contains nitrogen, which helps plants grow. Worm castings—or worm poop—also contains nutrients that are good for plants. But if worms are so small, how is it they do a big farm so much good? It's because there are so many of them. Up to one million worms can be found in just one acre of land!

Jeepers Creepers!

Ribbon worms can grow to be 90 feet long and have been known to . . .

a. form bows as they slither on the ground.
b. tie themselves into knots.
c. get so tangled up with other ribbon worms that they can't tell where one worm ends and another begins.
d. travel at speeds of up to 30 miles per hour.

Making Tracks: Sporting one pair of legs for each segment of its flat-looking body, the centipede, also called a hundred-legger, can have from 15 to nearly 200 pairs. Six-legged insects move three legs at a time, two on one side and one on the other—a routine that gives them their zigzag motion. Centipedes can move swiftly, using the same basic gait but on a much grander scale.

Making Waves: Even though they are called thousand-leggers, millipedes only have about the same number of legs as centipedes. Unlike centipedes, however, millipedes have two pairs of short legs on each body segment, and their legs are set below their rounded body rather than out to the side. Millipedes are slower than centipedes, and move ten or more pairs of legs at a time in a wavelike motion.

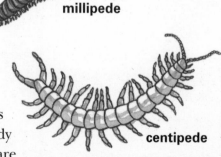

millipede

centipede

Bookworms? With no wings and a very flat body, the silverfish is perfectly suited for slithering into tight spaces. It's even been known to make itself at home between the pages of a book.

Flea for All: When it comes to jumping, fleas are the stars of the insect world. To jump as far as a flea, a person would have to jump the length of four football fields. The secret of the flea's amazing ability lies in a pad of *resilin,* a rubberlike material, above each of its heavily muscled back legs. As a flea gets ready to jump, it crouches, locking its hind legs against its body and tightly squeezing the resilin pads. When its legs snap free, the resilin releases the stored-up energy like a spring and catapults the flea high into the air.

Jeepers Creepers!

Which statement about scorpions is *not* true?

a. Scorpions can walk faster backward than they can forward.
b. Scorpions are weak fliers.
c. Scorpions often take off by jumping from a high elevation.
d. Scorpions have three sets of wings.

Step Right Up:

Imagine a circus in which all the participants are fleas. At one time, flea circuses were all the rage in Great Britain. A human ringmaster would use tweezers to lift the fleas, which were dressed in tiny clothing and harnessed by slender silver wires, onto a tightrope or miniature stage where they would juggle and ride teensy little bikes.

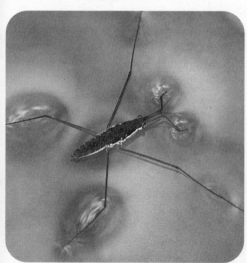

Skimming the Surface:

The water strider walks on water as easily as other bugs crawl on the ground. How does it do it? Molecules pulling on the surface of the water form a thin film. The water strider takes advantage of this by spreading its legs widely to support its weight evenly over the surface. Waterproof hairs on its legs also help keep it from breaking through the film.

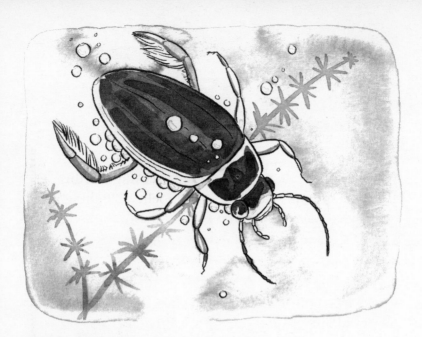

Scuba Bugs: The water beetle is able to spend most of its time underwater by storing air beneath its wings. The beetle breathes the air through tiny holes called *spiracles*. As the air supply is used up, the bubble acts like a kind of Aqua-Lung, taking in oxygen from the water.

Jeepers Creepers!

When the weather gets extremely hot, hopping grasshoppers cope by . . .

a. going for a swim.
b. moving along the ground at very high speeds.
c. growing a set of wings.
d. burrowing underground.

Brain Buster

Drive yourself buggy with these brain-busting activities as you try to separate fact from fiction!

Robert Ripley dedicated his life to seeking out the bizarre and unusual. But every unbelievable thing he recorded was known to be true. In the Brain Busters at the end of every chapter, you'll play Ripley's role—trying to verify the fantastic facts presented. Each Ripley's Brain Buster contains a group of four shocking statements. But of these so-called "facts," **one** is **fiction**. Will you **Believe It!** or **Not!**?

Wait—there's more! Following the Brain Busters are special bonus games where you can play "Who am I?" by trying to **Name That Bug!** Finally, tally your score by flipping to the end of the book for answer keys and a scorecard.

Crawly creatures have the oddest features. But can you spot the one bogus bug characteristic below? Yes, one of these four facts is purely fiction—but which one? You'll get 20 points if you can figure it out.

a. Saw-toothed grain beetles have jagged-edged teeth that allow them to chew—what else?—grain.

Believe It!   **Not!**

b. Praying mantises can rotate their heads 180 degrees to look over their shoulders, allowing them to hunt for food quite effectively.

Believe It!   **Not!**

c. Fireflies, who use their "tail lights" to attract mates, are the only order of insects that can produce light.

Believe It!   **Not!**

d. A darkling beetle actually stands on its head to drink. After dew forms on its back in the morning, the beetle tips its head forward so the water droplets roll down its back and into its mouth.

Believe It!   **Not!**

BONUS GAME—NAME THAT BUG!

If you've ever been bitten by me, you know how annoying I can be. I am the stable pest, especially outside in the sunshine. You can usually find me flying around a certain galloping animal. Sometimes, I admit, I do bite humans. But believe me, I'd much rather be sucking the blood of my big four-legged buddies.

Who am I?

— — — — — — — —

Bugs use sound, body language, and touch to communicate defensive, aggressive, or friendly behavior. But sometimes all they want to do is blend in.

Jeepers Creepers!

Some people think that if you count the number of chirps a cricket makes in 15 seconds and add 40, you can tell . . .

a. the air temperature.
b. the humidity.
c. how many hours until the next rainfall.
d. the number of stars you can see in the sky.

Love Songs: Bugs often attract mates with their songs. The male cicada uses a pair of special drumlike organs called *tymbals*. When the cicada contracts the muscles attached to the tymbals, they vibrate, producing the cicada's song. The song is amplified by a hollow section of the cicada's abdomen. Some cicadas can be heard for up to a quarter-mile away!

Food for Love: When he's ready to mate, a male scorpion fly catches a caterpillar, fly, or other juicy tidbit, then gives off a scent that will attract a female. When a female arrives, she inspects the male's gift—and it had better please her. Otherwise, she'll fly off in search of another mate who's caught something juicier.

Seeds of Love:

The male stinkbug sticks its pointed mouthparts into the kind of seed it likes to eat and holds it in place until a female stinkbug drops by. He gives her the seed and she lets him know that she appreciates his generosity by becoming his mate.

A Bug's-eye View

An insect's view of the world is very different from a human's.

The Better to See You: Each of a fly's compound eyes contains several thousand lenses. And each lens sees a slightly different image, making it highly unlikely that any morsel of food will go unnoticed.

Sights Unseen: Many insects can see ultraviolet light, which is completely invisible to humans.

What people see . . .

What a bee sees . . .

Seeing Eye to Eye: When two stalk-eyed flies cross paths, they compare eyes. The more distance between the male's eyes, the more attractive he is to the female of the species.

Snack Attack

In the bug world, sometimes you're the hunter and sometimes you're the meal.

Crawl and Maul: Some tarantulas can grow up to 11 inches wide. They feast on mice, frogs, lizards, birds, and snakes.

Lethal Beetle: Few insects are strong enough to catch vertebrates, but the diving beetle at left is having fish for lunch.

Mighty Bite: The bite of the Australian bulldog ant can be mildly poisonous to humans—but it's lethal to the bugs it likes to bite, butcher, and gobble up.

Take That!

Some bugs will go to great lengths to avoid becoming lunch.

Chemical Warfare: When the bombardier beetle (right) goes on the defensive, it lets loose a toxic squirt from its backside that makes even the fiercest predators run for cover.

Triple Threat: The puss moth caterpillar (left) is hard to see among the leaves. But if it is threatened, it puffs up its head and shows its horns. If that doesn't work, a little acid, sprayed from its tail, sends the would-be predator on its way.

Blood, Spit, and Tears: When under attack, the flightless bloody-nosed beetle spits out a drop of nasty-tasting blood, which scares its enemies or makes them sick.

Hide

For many insects, the best way to avoid becoming a meal is to blend in with their environment.

Stick Figure: Which is the walking stick bug and which is the twig?

In the Pink: The orchid mantis (below) looks like the flower it lives on. Can you tell the two apart?

Double Threat: With its wings closed, the peacock katydid of Peru (above) looks like a dead leaf, but when its cover is blown, it raises its wings to show off a pair of menacing snakelike eyes.

and Seek

Leaves a Puzzle: If you were a hungry bug looking for a bite to eat, would you be able to tell this was a yummy leaf insect and not an actual leaf?

The Yuck Factor: Since it looks like bird droppings, the caterpillar form of the giant swallowtail butterfly is not very appealing to predators.

Thorny Disguise: Who would want to step on, much less chomp on, a sharp thorn? Looking like a piece of a prickly plant has saved many a treehopper from becoming someone's lunch.

Bug Theater

Most bugs go through several stages before they become adults. This growing process is called metamorphosis.

Act 1: The female monarch butterfly finds a tender plant and lays her eggs.

Act 2: After the larvae (caterpillars) hatch from the eggs, they eat (and eat and eat), growing bigger and bigger.

Act 3: The fully grown caterpillar attaches itself upside down to a plant. Working from the head up, it starts to form a chrysalis.

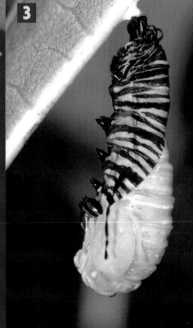

Act 4: When the pupa is almost fully developed, you can see the future butterfly's wings.

Act 5: At last the chrysalis splits open and the adult butterfly emerges, its wings still crumpled and wrinkly.

Act 6: After a few minutes, the butterfly's wings expand and smooth out. Soon it will be ready to fly away.

Bon Appétit!

Just about anything can end up on an insect's menu—even food that's still alive.

Tiny Vampires: The African tsetse fly bulks up on the blood of mammals—including humans—and often spreads disease.

Bug Hospitality: The ant protects the aphid from its enemies and, in return, gets honeydew nectar from the aphid. A relationship like this between two different species is called symbiosis.

Dining In: A parasitic wasp injects its eggs into a living caterpillar. After hatching, the wasp larvae eat their host alive, then burst through its skin, leaving nothing but cocoons behind.

Dinner Dance: Worker bees have a special way of communicating. When one of them finds nectar, it goes home to the hive and spreads the news by doing a waggle dance. The speed of the waggle tells the others how far they have to fly to find the food, while the angle of the waggle tells them where to find it.

That's Using Their Heads: To warn their housemates that danger is near, soldier termites bang their heads against the floors and ceilings of their burrows. The sound echoes throughout the nest, sending the termites scurrying away to safety.

Jeepers Creepers!

Which statement is *not* true?

a. In some countries, people collect fireflies in net bags to wear around their ankles to light their way.
b. The light from two carbuncle beetles placed in a jar is bright enough to read by.
c. Firefly lanterns can be found in some gardens in Japan.
d. Spiders are afraid of fireflies.

Heads, I Win; Tails, I Win: The bulldog ant of Australia is one the fiercest types of ant. Once it takes a bite with its strong jaws, called *mandibles*, it never lets go. If you cut a bulldog ant in half, the front will grab its own tail with its teeth and the tail will sting the head. The fight can last for quite a long time.

The Terminator: The longest of all beetles, the Hercules beetle can measure up to eight inches long, horns included. When males fight, they use their horns to pick up the enemy and fling it away.

Double Whammy: The enemies of fire ants—including people—should think twice before bothering these fierce little bugs. They hold on to their victim with their jaws and sting repeatedly, injecting an extremely painful venom.

News Flash: Fireflies are really beetles. They talk to each other by flashing their lights. The male flashes first in midair. Several seconds later, the female, who is often wingless, answers from the ground with her own light. Each species of firefly has its own signal that is recognized by others of its species. But some fireflies mimic the signal of another species to lure and eat any unlucky prey that falls for the trick.

Jeepers Creepers!

To confuse predators, some grasshoppers are able to adjust the angle of their forewings to . . .

a. throw their voices like ventriloquists.
b. mimic praying mantises.
c. blend into the foliage.
d. create the impression that they have huge jaws.

Little Stinkers:

Millipedes are vegetarians. To defend themselves against hunters, they squeeze out stinking juice from pores along the sides of their bodies. One whiff, and most predators will scatter.

Beetle Juice: The bloody-nosed beetle can't fly. Nor can it run very fast. But it has one bizarre defense mechanism that explains its name. When danger lurks, the bloody-nosed beetle squeezes out a drop of bright

red liquid to discourage anything that wants to take a bite out of it. This stuff looks nasty and tastes even worse.

Ready, Set, Squirt! When under threat of attack, the wood ant points its abdomen toward its enemy. As the predator comes closer, the wood ant sprays it with acid from the tip of its abdomen.

Jeepers Creepers!

Desert beetles can kill other insects with their . . .

a. venom.
b. claws.
c. stingers.
d. odor.

Pain-Stalking: Centipedes are predators equipped with poison glands. A bite from a centipede can cripple its prey. Centipedes are not considered dangerous to humans, but the bite of some of the large tropical species can be very painful.

Playing Dead: The click beetle tries to escape notice by lying on its back, perfectly still. But if it's attacked, it snaps its head up, hurtling itself away from danger and landing on its feet. The beetle gets its name from the clicking noise it makes when it snaps its head.

CLICK!

Escape Artists:

Why do flyswatters have holes in them? Because the holes lessen the air pressure—which flies can detect via the hairs on their legs—thus giving you a better chance to surprise the fly and make a direct hit!

Presto Change-o!

The puss moth caterpillar (*see color insert*) is a master of disguise. Its green color helps it blend in with leaves. But if spotted, it can puff out a bright red fold of skin around its head, complete with spots that resemble two fierce-looking eyes. And if the predator comes closer, the caterpillar can stick out its tail and spray it with formic acid.

Black and Blue: The black grasshopper of Australia turns sky blue as soon as the sun comes up.

Smoke Screen:
In 1850, natural history experts began to notice that the light-colored peppered moths that lived in industrial towns like Birmingham, England, had become darker in color. The scientists concluded that this

species of moth was forced to change, or *mutate,* along with its environment, which had become polluted with black soot. Moths in the countryside kept their original color.

Jeepers Creepers!

During the course of a summer, a katydid repeats its song about . . .

a. 50 million times.
b. 5,000 times.
c. 500,000 times.
d. 50,000 times.

Hiding in Plain Sight: Prey can barely see the cryptic tree bark spider when it rests on the tree bark it so closely resembles.

Heads or Tails? On each back wing, the hairstreak butterfly has markings that look a bit like a head and thin extensions that look like antennae. Predators have a hard time telling whether the butterfly is coming or going.

Nuts to You: The peanut bug has a hollow snout that looks like an unshelled peanut. If its head doesn't scare a predator away, the peanut bug opens it wings, revealing big red-and-black eye-shaped markings.

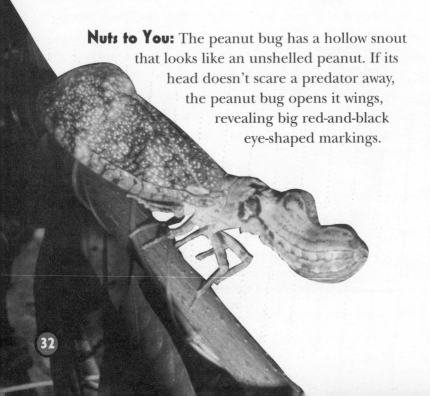

What a Hag!

For protection, the hag moth caterpillar doesn't just rely on looking like a dead leaf. It also has twisted black stinging hairs hidden among the brown hairs on its fleshy body.

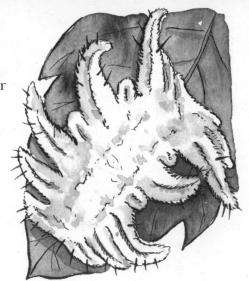

Hair-Raisers:

Fat, juicy caterpillars look yummy to most predators. But the hairs on their bodies make many caterpillars unfit for dinner. Some have hairs that are disgustingly sticky. Others have hairs or spines that are connected to poison glands and can even cause pain to humans. When touched, the spines of the puss caterpillar, for example, break off and release venom, causing swelling, a rash, and nausea.

Anti-Sonar Devices: Bats use a
form of sonar called *echolocation* to find the moths they love to eat. But some moths send out signals that are capable of jamming the bats' sound waves so that they can't determine the moths' locations.

Jeepers Creepers!

The male mole cricket's song is amplified by his burrow, and can be heard . . .

a. a half-mile away.
b. 100 feet away.
c. 1,000 feet away.
d. 50 yards away.

Hair Cuts:

Tarantulas that live in the Americas have barbed, bristlelike hairs on their abdomen called *urticating hairs*. When disturbed, they rub the hairs off with their back legs and send them flying at their attacker. If a small animal breathes in the hairs, its air passages may swell up so much that it suffocates.

Aphid Army:

With their tiny, soft bodies, most aphids are pretty defenseless—except for the Alexander's horned aphid. Some members of this species have a hard, armorlike body and sharp, swordlike mouthparts. To defend themselves, they band together and attack a predator, holding on to it with their strong front legs while stabbing it with their mouthparts.

Bitter Beetles:

When a predator notices the bright colors of ladybugs, it knows not to come near. Their striking coloration is a warning that these insects have a bitter taste and will make an attacker sick if it tries to eat them.

Jeepers Creepers!

To avoid being caught by bats, some moths . . .

a. play dead.
b. squirt venom.
c. fly backward.
d. chirp like birds.

Sticking Together: When predators come near, colonial caterpillars flip their bodies back and forth in a frantic frenzy. They stay so close to each other that the enemy thinks they are one big creature, and takes off in fright.

Built-in Survival Kit: With jaws strong enough to draw the blood of its enemies, and sharp, pointed spines, the spiny devil katydid is far from defenseless.

Roll Model: When threatened, the South African white lady spider doesn't stick around. Instead, it tucks in its legs and curls into a ball. Then away it rolls at breakneck speed, down sand dunes and far from predators.

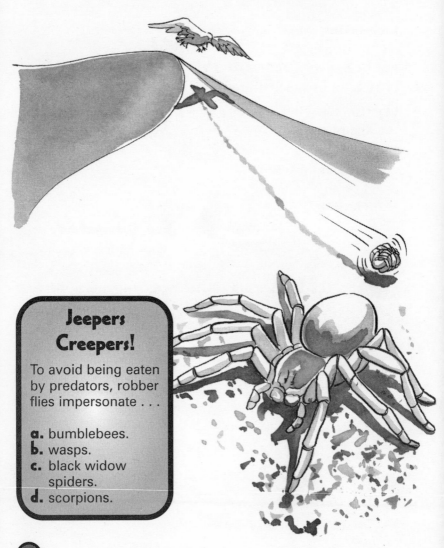

Jeepers Creepers!

To avoid being eaten by predators, robber flies impersonate . . .

a. bumblebees.
b. wasps.
c. black widow spiders.
d. scorpions.

You won't believe the bizarre names of certain bugs! But only three of the following incredible insects really exist. Can you find the phony?

a. The extraordinarily rare superfly got its name because of its super strength. Its muscle power rivals that of a small dog!

Believe It!   **Not!**

b. The confused flour beetle can be a pest of flourmills and grocery stores alike. (The "flour" part is clear, but what's the beetle so "confused" about?)

Believe It!   **Not!**

c. The acrobat ant looks like its doing a balancing act when it holds half its body up in the air.

Believe It!   **Not!**

d. The cucumber beetle loves to prey upon cucumbers in the garden.

Believe It!   **Not!**

BONUS GAME—NAME THAT BUG!

I am a hairy brown arachnid that looks pretty creepy.
Don't be fooled by my fast, aggressive movements—I am
really quite harmless. I don't spin webs like most of my
relatives. Instead, I hunt and capture my food. Though I
certainly can't make loud noises, I am named after a
mammal that howls.

Who am I?

__ __ __ __   __ __ __ __ __ __

Most bugs start out as eggs—and their parents have devised as many different ways to keep them safe as there are . . . well, bugs.

Jeepers Creepers!

Apple maggots produce chemicals that . . .

a. make their food tender enough to chew.
b. prevent a second female from laying eggs on fruit they already occupy.
c. keep birds away.
d. glue themselves to their perch.

Eggs-tremely Secure: Malacosoma moths lay strings of eggs that they wind around the limbs of fruit trees. The eggs are so tightly glued that the heaviest of storms cannot wash them away.

Eggs-tra Protection: A female cockroach lays hard little purselike cases. Inside each case are batches of eggs. When the wingless baby cockroaches, called *nymphs,* hatch, they look very much like their parents.

No Stalking Allowed:

Green lacewings lay each of their eggs at the end of a long, hairlike stalk. Out of reach, the eggs remain safe from small predators until hatching time.

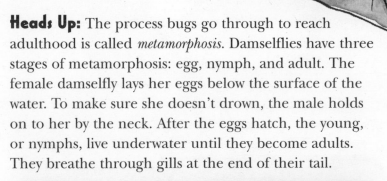

Heads Up: The process bugs go through to reach adulthood is called *metamorphosis.* Damselflies have three stages of metamorphosis: egg, nymph, and adult. The female damselfly lays her eggs below the surface of the water. To make sure she doesn't drown, the male holds on to her by the neck. After the eggs hatch, the young, or nymphs, live underwater until they become adults. They breathe through gills at the end of their tail.

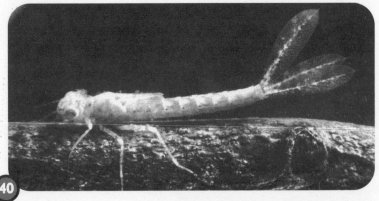

Just a Stage: Many insects go through complete metamorphosis, which involves four stages. They start as eggs. When the young, called *larvae*, hatch, they do nothing but eat and grow. Moth larvae are called caterpillars. To prepare for the third stage, *pupation*, the caterpillars produce a silk cocoon to wrap themselves in. While inside, the caterpillars develop into adults, and eventually emerge as moths. For a step-by-step guide to the metamorphosis of a butterfly, check out the color insert!

Jeepers Creepers!

Some people believe that they can predict how long winter will last by finding a woolly caterpillar and measuring . . .

a. how long it is.
b. its weight.
c. the length of its brown middle.
d. how thick its "wool" is.

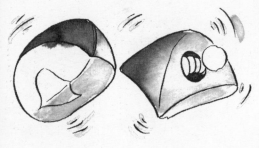

Mexican Jumping Bean: No, jumping beans don't really jump. After it hatches, the caterpillar of a small species of moth bores its way into the young seed of a bush. It eats the inside of the seed, then builds a web in the hollow shell. When the seed falls off the bush, the caterpillar flings itself from one side to the other, moving the bean and making it look as though it's jumping. The warmer the weather, the more the caterpillar moves around. When the caterpillar becomes a pupa, it stops moving. Months later, the adult moth chews a hole in the seed and flies away.

Deep Freeze: Cabbage butterflies spend winters in their pupa stage. A substance called *glycerol* in their body fluid acts as a kind of antifreeze, keeping the water inside the insect's cells from freezing and rupturing the cell membranes. Drops of glycerol seep through the cell walls so that ice forms outside the cells instead of inside. The glycerol causes the ice to form without jagged edges, giving added protection.

Jeepers Creepers!

The swallowtail caterpillar is usually left alone because of . . .

a. its bad taste.
b. its long, sticky tongue.
c. the hissing sound it makes.
d. the two large eyespots on its back.

From Grave to Cradle: At night, burying beetles use their remarkable sense of smell to locate newly dead birds, mice, and other small animals. If a male finds one, he sits on it and

either waits for a female to arrive or gives off a chemical to attract her. The two beetles then dig a hole under the corpse to bury it. Next, they strip the body of fur or feathers, roll it into a ball, and spray it with a fluid that helps preserve it. Finally, the female lays her eggs nearby. After hatching, the larvae, or grubs, can munch on the corpse or eat food that the parents throw up. Both parents stick around, keeping the corpse free of fungus and bacteria until the grubs are ready to pupate.

Hatchbacks: When a female giant water bug sees a male water bug that looks healthy and strong, she goes after him. After she catches him, she lays her eggs on his back, securing them with a special glue secreted from her body. The male water

bug has no choice but to carry the eggs around with him until they hatch.

43

Stock Pot: Each egg of the potter wasp gets its own little pot to protect it. The female wasp takes several hours to fashion a pot out of mud. Then she finds a juicy caterpillar, paralyzes it with her stinger, and stuffs it into the pot. Finally, she lays one egg in the pot and stops it up with more mud. Once the egg hatches, the larva has a caterpillar feast.

Playing Favorites: Scientists can't explain how, but potter wasp mothers know which eggs are male and which are female. For some reason, the males get smaller pots and less food than the females.

Dry Idea: Dragonflies lay their eggs in or near water. To keep from getting wet, these clever insects sometimes stand on water-lily pads while laying their eggs. Some dragonflies simply drop their eggs as they fly over the water. After the eggs hatch, the larvae may live underwater for several years.

Up, Up, and Away:

Some newly hatched spiders leave home by ballooning. First, they stand on tiptoe. Next, they spin a long silk line that drifts out behind them. Then, as soon as a breeze catches the strand of silk, they ride it until they land in a good spot to begin their new lives.

Jeepers Creepers!

In the first hour after a bee is born, it is fed . . .

a. hundreds of regurgitated worms.
b. watered-down honey.
c. crushed insects.
d. 500 times.

Pooper-Scoopers: Like potter wasps, dung beetles go to a lot of trouble to protect their eggs. But instead of using mud, they scout out fresh mammal droppings and roll the dung into a ball. Then they poke a hole in the ball to lay their eggs in it. When the eggs hatch, the larvae have to eat through the dung to get out.

Mommy Dearest:

One kind of spider wasp will do anything for her offspring—even attack a much larger tarantula. Though an adult tarantula hawk wasp eats nothing but nectar, her larvae need meat to grow. So before she lays an egg, the mother wasp lures a tarantula out of its burrow and paralyzes it with her poisonous stinger. Then she digs a burrow, drags the spider inside, lays an egg on its abdomen, and plugs up the hole. When the larva hatches, its dinner is ready and waiting.

Hitching a Ride:

Instead of building a web, the female wolf spider wraps her eggs in a sac and carries them around with her to protect them. After they hatch, the baby spiders live on their mother's back until they are old enough to hunt on their own.

Full Cycle:

In early spring, aphid eggs hatch into wingless females that are already pregnant! Throughout the spring and summer, many generations of winged and wingless females are born, but it's not until fall that male aphids arrive. These winged males mate with wingless females, who lay the eggs that will hatch the following spring— and begin the cycle all over again.

Jeepers Creepers!

The largest land-dwelling animal on the continent of Antarctica is the . . .

a. polar bear.
b. wingless midge.
c. snow flea.
d. emperor penguin.

Eggs-tremely Protective:

Shield bugs are one of the very few types of insects that defend their eggs after they've laid them. If an enemy ventures too close to her nest, the mother will do her best to scare it away.

Blood Sisters: Male mosquitoes feed on flower nectar. Female mosquitoes feed on the blood of humans and other mammals. Without blood, a female mosquito's eggs will not develop.

Jeepers Creepers!

One type of insect lives in the ground for 17 years before reaching adulthood. Sometimes called the 17-year locust, it is really a . . .

a. great golden digger wasp.
b. desert-burrowing cockroach.
c. periodical cicada.
d. gladiator katydid.

Biting Story: Even though we say we have a mosquito "bite," we really don't. The mosquito doesn't bite, but pierces the skin with her long mouthpart, called a *proboscis,* then uses it to suck up the blood.

What a cute baby! Err . . . maybe not. Bugs'
larval forms are unusual and distinct—but cute?
Not really. Of the following four curious bug baby
statements, can you spot the one that's just
kidding around?

a. After mosquito larvae hatch in a pond, they collect
food by filtering water through their mouth. In a single
day, these tiny creatures can each filter about one liter
of water!

Believe It!   **Not!**

b. Acorn weevil larvae actually develop inside an acorn,
feeding on the nutmeat for about three weeks.

Believe It!   **Not!**

c. The scent of stinkbug nymphs is so powerful that
they are offended by their own stench. They try to wash
it off, but soon find out they are stuck with the smell
for life.

Believe It!   **Not!**

d. The larvae of Asian lady beetles, a type of ladybug,
are usually red and black and shaped like tiny
alligators.

Believe It!   **Not!**

BONUS QUESTION—NAME THAT BUG!

I am a true insect with a hard shell, and I live throughout North America. You can usually find me hovering around outdoor lights, particularly in the beginning of the summer. In fact, people got so used to seeing me then that they named me after the month in which summer begins.

Who am I?

__ __ __ __   __ __ __ __ __ __

4 Bug Buffet

Plants, insects, fish, birds, even shoe polish—if it can be digested, chances are it will wind up on some bug's menu.

Spitting It Out: The spitting spider has silk glands connected to its venom glands. This night-hunter can't see very well, but it has long hairs on its front legs that help it sense when prey is near. Then it creeps up and spits out two streams of venomous silk in a zigzag pattern, immobilizing its unsuspecting victim.

Jeepers Creepers!

The saliva of leeches contains a substance called *hirudin* that is helpful to humans because it . . .

a. builds up red blood cells.
b. cures indigestion.
c. fights bacteria.
d. slows blood clotting.

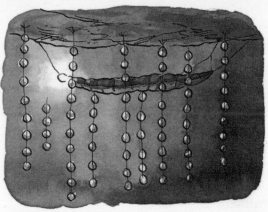

Cave Cuisine:

The larvae of fungus gnats in New Zealand have a special way to attract their dinner. They hang out in caves, where they glow in the dark. But that's not all. The larvae spin silken threads, add sticky spit, and dangle the threads below them. As insects fly toward the light, they get caught in the threads. The larvae pull up their threads and have a feast. Yum!

Mouthwatering Experience:

Before it can eat, a housefly must turn its food into liquid. To do this, the fly spits digestive juices onto its food, then soaks up the liquid with spongelike pads on its proboscis. After the fly leaves, you can sometimes see the spots left by the dried-up juices.

Jeepers Creepers!

Dung beetles were used by the Ancient Egyptians . . .

a. to make scarab jewelry.
b. to make rattles for babies.
c. as live toys for their favorite cats.
d. as decorations for coffins.

Waste Not, Want Not: One kind of termite in Africa has gardens inside its mound. Worker termites grow a special kind of fungus in their own droppings. The fungus breaks down the undigested cellulose

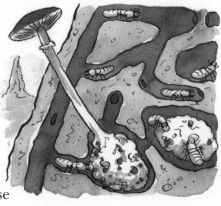

from the wood the termites eat. When the fungus—which is more easily digested than wood—is harvested, it's fed to the queen and king as well as the younger termites. As an added bonus, heat from the gardens helps keep air circulating through the mound.

Lip Service: Unlike its parents, a dragonfly nymph lives underwater. It catches the tadpoles and small fish it likes to eat with a hinged lower lip operated by its own blood pressure. When the nymph isn't hunting, it folds and tucks its lip extension under its head and thorax. But as soon as something tasty swims by, watch out! In less than a second, out shoots the lip. Two pincers at the end snag the prey and pull it in for a tasty treat.

Gotcha! Instead of spinning a web, the trapdoor spider builds a burrow with, yes, a trapdoor. The burrow is about six inches deep. The trapdoor is made of dirt and is attached to the side of the burrow with silk that the spider spins. The spider camouflages the door with leaves, sticks, and small stones. Then it hides under the door, waiting for prey to come along. When the spider hears an insect on the other side, it jumps out, grabs the bug, and pulls it into the burrow.

Tongue in Cheek:

Hawk moths have extremely long, slender tongues that they keep tucked away until it's time to feed. Uncoiled, the hawk moth's tongue can measure as long as 13 inches—
perfect for reaching deep inside flowers to get the nectar they like to drink.

Forward . . . March!

South American army ants live in colonies of up to one million. The blind worker ants use their own bodies to form the nest, called a *bivouac*. When swarms of army ants are on the march, they eat all the bugs in their path—up

to 100,000 in a single day. The worker ants are protected by soldier ants, which have such big jaws they can only eat if the workers feed them. In Africa, relatives of army ants are called driver ants. When they sweep through a village, everyone leaves. Inconvenient, perhaps, but after the driver ants move on, the people get to return to a bug-free village!

Buddy System:

Ants and aphids have a good thing going. The ants protect the aphids by eating the eggs of ladybugs and lacewings, whose larvae are aphid predators. Ants also let slow-going aphids hitch rides on their backs. To reward themselves, ants

Jeepers Creepers!

In 1479, the larvae of click beetles were tried and found guilty by the bishop of Lausanne, Switzerland, for the crime of . . .

a. carrying the plague.
b. eating stored grain.
c. devouring all the leaves on the trees.
d. eating all the crops.

milk aphids to get the sugary honeydew they produce. When two different species cooperate in this way, it's called *symbiosis*. (*See color insert.*)

Fungus Farm: Leaf-cutter ants have a well-developed system for producing their own food. First, worker ants cut off bits of leaves. Then smaller ants hop onto the leaves and guard against predators while the workers carry them back to the nest. The workers drop off the leaves at the entrance, where soldier ants with huge heads and fierce-looking jaws stand guard. Another group of worker ants carries the leaves underground, where they chew them up into a pulpy mass. This serves as a compost heap to grow the fungus that leaf-cutter ants need to thrive.

Web Sites: Many spiders spin webs to trap their prey. The webs are made from silk that the spider releases through tiny spigots called *spinnerets* on the back of its abdomen. The silk comes out as a liquid, but hardens as the spinnerets work like tiny fingers to weave the silk into the kind of web the particular spider weaves. Different types of webs include the orb web, the hammock web, the funnel web, and the sheet web.

It's a Wrap: Not all silk is used for webs. Spiders use different types of silk from different glands to protect their eggs, to make draglines so they can travel, and to hunt prey. Still another type of silk is used for storing food. If a spider is not going to eat its prey right away, it saves it by wrapping it up in hundreds of silken threads spun from its own special wrapping gland.

Target Practice: Orb webs look like beautifully constructed lace doilies and take about an hour to make. Since the webs are visible to insects, why don't they just fly around them? Scientists think that some webs may have the same kind of ultraviolet patterns that attract insects to flowers—which would explain why so many insects get caught in them!

Jeepers Creepers!

Silk clothing is made from a type of . . .

a. spider web.
b. caterpillar cocoon.
c. moth antenna.
d. butterfly wing.

Bungee Jumping Champion: When a jumping spider spots a potential meal, it attaches a silk dragline to its jumping-off point and leaps onto its prey. The dragline also serves as a lifeline in case the spider misses or needs to make a quick getaway. Some jumping spiders can leap 25 or more times their own body length.

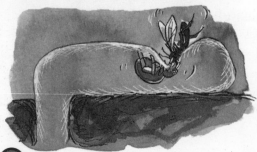

In the Bag:

The purse web spider spins itself a pouch of silk and stays inside waiting for an insect to land on it. Then it bites through the pouch to kill the unsuspecting bug before it knows what hit it.

Fast Food: The ogre-faced spider lives in tropical forests. At night, it hangs upside down just above the ground, holding a small sticky web with its four front legs. When a tasty morsel comes along, the spider hurls the web like a net to capture a midnight snack.

Jeepers Creepers!

Considered a sign of good luck, in some Middle Eastern countries spiders are . . .

a. placed in bassinets of newborn babies.
b. worn in the hair.
c. placed in the bed of newlywed couples.
d. given to children on their first day of school.

Armed and Dangerous: When they're not hiding from enemies by pretending to be bird droppings, bolas spiders have a unique way of hunting. They spin a silken thread with a glob of sticky stuff at one end. Holding onto the other end, they fling the thread to catch their prey and reel it in.

Vise Squad: Praying mantises count on the element of surprise. Great at blending in with its environment, a mantis balances on its back four legs and waits for prey to come near. Then, in a fraction of a second, it flicks out its barbed front legs and snaps them shut, holding its victim in a viselike grip. It's not uncommon for the mantis to eat another mantis, or to begin devouring its prey while it's still struggling to get away.

Sucking Up: The tear moth of Southeast Asia quenches its thirst in quite an unusual way. It lands and makes itself comfortable near the eye of a large mammal such as a buffalo. Then it inserts its long proboscis into the animal's eye and drinks its tears. The proboscis is so thin that it can slip under the eyelid of a sleeping animal without waking it up.

Jeepers Creepers!

Although it eats many different kinds of insects, a praying mantis will never eat . . .

a. a dragonfly.
b. a wasp.
c. an ant.
d. a bumblebee.

Thanks for Sharing:

Honey-pot ants live in desert areas and have an ingenious way to keep from starving when food is scarce. Storage ants called *repletes* are fed huge quantities of nectar. Barely able to move, they hang from the ceiling of the nest. If the repletes get too full, they will pop like little yellow balloons. But if the colony has trouble finding food, they need look no further than the storage ants. These obliging creatures will throw up all they have eaten so that the rest of the ants can have a meal.

Not Too Picky:

Cockroaches have been around for millions of years. Maybe it's because roaches will eat almost anything, from food scraps to cardboard to shoe polish to their own offspring. On the other hand, they can go for months without eating. If you cut off a roach's head, it can live for a week. The only reason it doesn't live longer is because it dies of thirst.

Liquid Lunch: The assassin bug hides and lies in wait for its prey. Then it strikes out with its beak, stabbing its victim and injecting it with venom. The chemicals dissolve the victim's insides so that they can be easily slurped up.

Fooling Around:

The ant-nest beetle lives among wood ants. The beetle tricks the ants into feeding it by giving off a chemical that makes it smell just like its hosts.

Jeepers Creepers!

Scientists can measure the amount of pollution in the atmosphere by . . .

a. studying bee pollen.
b. analyzing spider webs.
c. sifting through termite nests.
d. counting the flashes of fireflies.

Brain Buster

What's for dinner? If you're a bug, it could be just about anything. Can you tell which of these four gourmet bug stories has been cooked up just for you?

a. The wee harlequin beetle, a member of the stinkbug family, is known for its love of asparagus.
Believe It!   **Not!**

b. Talk about going hungry! Cecropia moths only live about two weeks because, in their adult form, they cannot eat. They don't even have a mouth or proboscis!
Believe It!   **Not!**

c. The antlion gets its name because, in its larval form, it loves to devour ants.
Believe It!   **Not!**

d. What picky eaters! When lurking in closets, moths actually prefer to chew on expensive designer clothes.
Believe It!   **Not!**

BONUS GAME—NAME THAT BUG!

I am a black-and-yellow striped beetle that lives primarily in western regions of North America. My name comes from the food I eat—I am a vegetable-crop pest that loves to feed on the plant of a certain brown, round, under-the-ground vegetable.

Who am I?

— — — — —   — — —

Insect homes come in all shapes and sizes, from the simplest leaf to the most complex underground burrow.

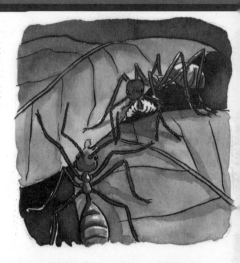

Child Labor: Tailor ants, also known as weaver ants, make their nests in the leaves of trees. While some worker ants pull the edges of the leaves together, others move along, each holding an ant larva in its jaws and squeezing until the larva releases a bit of the same silk it will later use to build its cocoon. As the sticky silk dries, it glues the leaves tightly together.

Jeepers Creepers!

Leaf-cutter ants are such great escape artists that zookeepers have to . . .

a. coat the walls of their glass cages with slippery chemicals.
b. make their cages out of the finest iron mesh.
c. surround their cages with poisonous snakes.
d. cover their feet with Vaseline.

Construction Paper:

Like bees, social wasps live and work within a group. To build their nests, they make a paperlike substance by chewing on wood fibers. You've probably seen the large, gray, egg-shaped nests of the North American bald-faced hornets (which are really wasps) hanging from a tree branch or under the eaves of a building. Try looking at the nest with binoculars and see if you can spot streaks of color. If the wasps chewed on wood that was painted, their nest will be streaked with whatever color was on the wood!

Bug in a Bubble: The water spider spins its underwater nest from silk, then stocks it with air. Tiny hairs on the spider's abdomen help it carry air bubbles down from the surface. After it traps enough air under the silk, it settles down to wait for prey. When something tasty happens along, the water spider attacks and brings its meal back into its comfy, air-filled web to eat.

Astounding Mounds: It takes the fungus-growing termites that live in the tropical grasslands of Africa years to construct their homes, which can reach 20 feet high. These towers, built out of saliva and either sand, clay, or sawdust, feature elaborate networks of interlacing tunnels. At the center of each mound are fungus gardens, and hidden deep within is the royal chamber, home to the king and queen. The queen may lay up to 30,000 eggs a day, providing enough soldier and worker termites to keep the whole operation running smoothly.

Jeepers Creepers!

Scientists think that some termite mounds may have been inhabited . . .

a. for more than 4,000 years.
b. by monkeys.
c. as fortresses.
d. by humans.

Bee-hemoth: Under cliffs in the Himalayan Mountains, giant honeybees build honeycombs that measure up to seven feet long and weigh up to 400 pounds.

Keeping Their Cool: Bees build hives of wax consisting of individual six-sided cells. The wax is produced by the bees themselves. In extreme heat, bees have several ways to air-condition their hive. One way is to beat their wings like fans, sending currents of air throughout the hive. Another way is to plug up openings in empty cells with water or diluted honey. As the liquid evaporates, it cools the air.

Hide-and-Seek: The nymphs of froghopper bugs—also called spittlebugs—love to eat plant sap. But most plants are teaming with predators that love to eat froghopper nymphs! The solution? The nymphs cover themselves with

frothy bubbles that look like spit. The froth consists of air mixed with liquids that are secreted from the nymphs' rear end and abdomen.

Petal Palace: In Central and South America, some ants carry seeds into their nest. In time, they sprout, making the nest look like a tiny flower garden.

Jeepers Creepers!

In a beehive, there can never be more than one queen. When the old queen dies, the new queen emerges from her cocoon and . . .

a. seals the door of her cell with a special glue.
b. stabs her sisters to death with her stinger.
c. immediately lays 5,000 eggs.
d. drinks all the honey.

Tomb and Gloom: Bees are far from hospitable to uninvited guests. If a creature such as a mouse accidentally drops by the hive, the bees band together and sting it to death. Then they go outside and gather sticky material that can be found on plants and twigs. They use the sticky stuff to bind the corpse like a mummy. When it dries and hardens, the intruder is left where it died, entombed in the hive.

Mobile Home:
The caddis fly larva lives underwater in a tube-shaped mobile home it builds for itself. It uses sand and bits of leaves and sticks, which it glues together with spit. Only the larva's head is visible, peering out from one end as it creeps along the bottom of the pond.

Bag It: The Colletes bee makes an underground nest with a tiny cell for each of her eggs. To protect them, she lines the cells with a polyester-like substance she excretes from a special gland. Then she fills the cells with food for the

larvae to eat when they hatch. Scientists who have analyzed the substance have found that, although it is not woven, it is essentially the same as the manufactured polyester used in clothing.

Mini Apartment Houses: The female carpenter bee drills a tunnel a little less than a foot long inside a broken twig—quite a feat for such a tiny creature. To equal the effort, a human would have to dig a hole 200 feet deep by hand. The bee lines the inside of her tunnel with several pollen-filled layers, separated from each other by a partition. Each little apartment contains one egg. When the eggs hatch, the baby bees eat the pollen and chew their way to freedom.

Jeepers Creepers!

A type of European bee makes its nest in the empty shells of . . .

a. crayfish.
b. bird eggs.
c. snails.
d. turtles.

On a Roll:

Leaf-rolling weevils and their distinctive nests, which hang from trees like miniature, green-colored egg rolls, can be found throughout the world. These tiny beetles cut leaves in precise ways to make their nests. The weevil notches each side of a leaf

near the stem from the outside edge to the middle. As soon as the leaf wilts, the weevil presses the two sides together. Then, starting from the tip, the weevil rolls the leaf back toward its body, makes a slit, and lays its egg inside. After sealing in the egg, the weevil finishes rolling the leaf up. When the larva hatches, it gets out by eating its way through the layers of leaf.

Jeepers Creepers!

The homes of cathedral termites in Australia are . . .

a. filled with praying mantises.
b. air-conditioned by a series of tunnels.
c. lit by fireflies.
d. decorated with feathers and shells.

Hives, holes, and nests . . . there are all kinds of places that bugs call home. But don't let these four homey details deceive you. One of these bug abodes is bogus.

a. Earwigs can survive in any crevice or small space, but they prefer to live in certain animals' ear canals.
Believe It!   Not!

b. Pecans are in serious danger when shuckworms are around. This worm tunnels in and makes its home inside the nut, preventing it from developing properly.
Believe It!   Not!

c. The cigarette beetle often makes its home in tobacco farms and manufacturing facilities, since it likes to feed on dried, stored tobacco.
Believe It!   Not!

d. One super colony of ants in Japan spanned an area of about 1.7 miles. The colony is reported to have had more than one million queens and more than 300 million worker ants.
Believe It!   Not!

BONUS GAME—NAME THAT BUG!

I am commonly mistaken for a spider, but I am really a close relative known as a harvestman. My legs are thinner and longer than a spider's, and I only have one body section instead of two. People often think I'm poisonous and get scared when they find me in their basement. But the truth is, I am totally harmless. In fact, there's something *parental* about me . . .

Who am I?

_ _ _ _ _   _ _ _ _ _ _ _ _ _

POP QUIZ

This section is crawling with score-builders—it's time for the official Pest Test! Have you caught all the bizarre bug facts in this book? Well, investigate your insect insight with this quiz. Pencils ready?

1. Which of the following is *not* a true bug?
a. Aphid
b. Treehopper
c. Pondstrider
d. Maggot

2. Molting occurs when . . .
a. a bug outgrows its exoskeleton.
b. tree bark peels off after certain bug infestations.
c. a bug starts eating its way out of a cocoon.
d. termites invade a building.

3. Insect antennae are *not* used to . . .
a. see.
b. smell.
c. hear.
d. sense temperature.

4. The Australian cockroach bites off its antennae when it reaches full maturity.
        Believe It!   **Not!**

5. Which of the following buggy-love stories is *not* true?

a. Scorpion flies woo their mates with insect gifts.

b. Cicadas use drumlike organs to sing to their honeys.

c. Female graffiti bugs attract a mate's attention by carving symbols into wooden porches and steps.

d. Female water bugs mate with big strong hunks—then let them carry the fertilized eggs on their back.

6. Some insects taste foul in order to discourage predators from attacking. Can you spot the insect that makes a particularly sickening snack?

a. Ladybug

b. Cricket

c. Stinkbug

d. Termite

7. When an insect undergoes complete metamorphosis, it passes through four stages. What is the correct order?

a. Egg, larva, pupa, adult.

b. Larva, egg, pupa, adult.

c. Pupa, adult, egg, larva.

d. Egg, larva, adult, pupa.

8. Some insects protect their eggs by wrapping them up. Can you tell which one of these three statements is egg-straordinarily *un*true?

a. Dung beetles lay their eggs in balls of dung.

b. Wolf spiders carry their eggs around with them, safe inside a sac.

c. Purse ants weave tiny purses out of grass to keep their eggs safe.

d. Potter wasps lay their eggs in tiny mud pots.

9. A certain kind of moth actually drinks tears from a sleeping animal's eyes.

Believe It!   **Not!**

10. A housefly eats its meals in which of the following amazing methods?

a. By smashing the food between its wings.

b. By decomposing the food in a covering of fungus.

c. By landing upon the food and sucking it up through its hollow legs.

d. By liquefying the food with spit.

11. Spiders use their silk in all kinds of cool ways. But one of these four uses is nothing but a yarn. Can you spot it?

a. Storing food

b. Communicating

c. Traveling

d. Protecting their eggs

12. A cockroach can live for a week without its head. Eventually, it dies because of . . .

a. dehydration.

b. starvation.

c. coldness.

d. boredom.

13. Some wasps regurgitate wood fibers to build their nests, which can have brightly colored streaks if the wasp has been chewing on painted wood.

Believe It!   **Not!**

14. Fungus-growing termites in Africa construct homes that can be as tall as . . .

a. 5 feet.

b. 10 feet.

c. 15 feet.

d. 20 feet.

15. Three of the following bee statements are buzzing with truth. Which one is pure make *bee*-lieve?

a. Bees may kill and entomb uninvited guests who enter the hive.

b. Bee babies spend their first 12 hours living underwater.

c. Bees may keep the hive cool by beating their wings to act as fans.

d. Giant honeybees have built hives that weigh as much as 400 pounds.

Answer Key

Chapter 1
Creature Features

Page 5:   **b.** 200 million insects.
Page 7:   **b.** a black lens.
Page 8:   **d.** clear or pale yellow or green.
Page 10:   **a.** In some parts of Africa, children tie strings to goliath beetles and keep them as pets.
Page 13:   **a.** scales that reflect light.
Page 14:   **a.** can walk through red-hot ashes.
Page 16:   **b.** tie themselves into knots.
Page 18:   **d.** Scorpions have three sets of wings.
Page 20:   **c.** growing a set of wings.
Brain Buster: c. is false.
Bonus Game: horse fly

Chapter 2
Going Buggy

Page 23:   **a.** the air temperature.
Page 25:   **d.** Spiders are afraid of fireflies.
Page 27:   **a.** throw their voices like ventriloquists.
Page 29:   **d.** odor.
Page 31:   **a.** 50 million times.
Page 33:   **a.** a half-mile away.
Page 34:   **a.** play dead.
Page 36:   **a.** bumblebees.
Brain Buster: a. is false.
Bonus Game: wolf spider

Chapter 3

Bug Babies

Page 39:   **b.** prevent a second female from laying eggs on fruit they already occupy.

Page 41:   **c.** the length of its brown middle.

Page 42:   **d.** the two large eyespots on its back.

Page 45:   **d.** 500 times.

Page 47:   **b.** wingless midge.

Page 48:   **c.** periodical cicada.

Brain Buster: c. is false.

Bonus Game: June beetle

Chapter 4

Bug Buffet

Page 51:   **d.** slows blood clotting.

Page 52:   **a.** to make scarab jewelry.

Page 55:   **d.** eating all the crops.

Page 57:   **b.** caterpillar cocoon.

Page 59:   **c.** placed in the bed of newlywed couples.

Page 60:   **c.** an ant.

Page 62:   **a.** studying bee pollen.

Brain Buster: d. is false.

Bonus Game: potato bug

Chapter 5
Bug Abodes
Page 65:   **a.** coat the walls of their glass cages with slippery chemicals.

Page 67:   **a.** for more than 4,000 years.

Page 69:   **b.** stabs her sisters to death with her stinger.

Page 71:   **c.** snails.

Page 72:   **b.** air-conditioned by a series of tunnels.

Brain Buster: a. is false.

Bonus Game: daddy longlegs

Pop Quiz

1.   **d.**
2.   **a.**
3.   **a.**
4.   **Not!**
5.   **c.**
6.   **a.**
7.   **a.**
8.   **c.**
9.   **Believe It!**
10. **d.**
11. **b.**
12. **a.**
13. **Believe It!**
14. **d.**
15. **b.**

What's Your Ripley's Rank?

Ripley's Scorecard

Well done! Your brain is a-buzzing with unbelievable bug facts! Now it's time to tally up your answers and get your Ripley's rating. Have you got **Insect Insight**? Or maybe you're **Bugging Out**? Add up your scores to find out!

Here's the scoring breakdown. Give yourself:
★ **10 points** for every **Jeepers Creepers!** you answered correctly;
★ **20 points** for every fiction you spotted in the **Ripley's Brain Busters**;
★ **10 points** for every time you were able to **Name That Bug!**;
★ and **5** for every **Pop Quiz** question you got right.

Here's a tally sheet:
Number of **Jeepers Creepers!**
questions answered correctly: _____ x 10 = _____

Number of **Ripley's Brain Buster**
fictions spotted: _____ x 20 = _____

Number of **Name That Bug!**
riddles solved: _____ x 10 = _____

Number of **Pop Quiz** questions
answered correctly: _____ x 5 = _____

Total the right column for your final score: _____

0-100
Something's buzzing . . .

. . . and it's the bug world. You know, those little crawly things you might have noticed all around you? Okay, so bugs aren't really your thing. That's all right. There are lots of other strange and unusual Ripley's facts to bug out about. Why not pick up some other zany Ripley books like *World's Weirdest Gadgets* or *Odd-inary People*?

101-250
Insect Insight

You're starting to get the bug! The unbelievable world of insects is luring you in slowly but surely. Don't be shy! Stand up and shout it loud and clear that the bug world is the best! All those amazing abilities and unlikely talents . . . just thinking about it is enough to make your head buzz. So many bugs, so little time to learn about them all!

251-400
Crawling with Knowledge

You've got this bug thing down! Your brain is crawling with all kinds of insect smarts—and you're not afraid to use 'em. Not only have you got a sense for the strange, you are perceptive in telling the difference between phony facts and remarkable realities. You might miss one here and there, but hey, nobody's perfect, right? Keep up the creepy-crawly curiosity.

401-575
Bugging Out!

Yep, you've definitely been bitten. You know more about the insect kingdom than may be good for you. (Unless of course, you plan on becoming an entomologist!) Eight-inch-long beetles, one million–member ant colonies, and poisonous silk-spitting spiders—this stuff is no big deal to *you*. And to top it all off, you've got a great eye for separating fact from fiction. Robert Ripley would be proud, even if your family might be a bit freaked out.

Believe It!®

Photo Credits

Ripley Entertainment Inc. and the editors of this book wish to thank the following photographers, agents, and other individuals for permission to use and reprint the following photographs in this book. Any photographs included in this book that are not acknowledged below are property of the Ripley Archives. Great effort has been made to obtain permission from the owners of all materials included in this book. Any errors that may have been made are unintentional and will gladly be corrected in future printings if notice is sent to Ripley Entertainment Inc., 5728 Major Boulevard, Orlando, Florida 32819.

Black & White Photos

6 Cicada/Greg Neise/www.geneise.com

7 Compound Eye/Microscope and Graphic Imaging Center, California State University, Hayward

8 Whirligig Beetles/Gary Meszaros/Bruce Coleman, Inc.

11 Long-horned Beetle; 26 Hercules Beetle/ Educational Images Ltd., Elmira, NY. All rights reserved. Used by permission.

13 Hooks on Bee's Wing; 24 Stinkbugs; 69 Froghopper Nymph/Ron West/Educational Images Ltd., Elmira, NY. All rights reserved. Used by permission.

14 Monarch Butterflies/Stephen Buchmann

17 Giant Centipede; 34 Tarantula; 67 Termite Mound/David Glynne Fox

19 Water Strider/Charles S. Lewallen

28 Bombardier Beetle/Thomas Eisner, Daniel Aneshansley, Cornell University

31 Cryptic Tree Bark Spider/Jeffrey W. Foltz

32 Peanut Bug; 55 Army Ants/Gerald R. Urquhart

40 Damselfly Nymph; 45 Dung Beetle/Csiro

43 Giant Water Bug with Eggs (*Abedus indentatus*) © Gerald & Buff Corsi/Visuals Unlimited

46 Wolf Spider; 57 Argiope Spider/Ed Nieuwenhuys

53 Dragonfly Nymph/John Mitchell/Photo Researchers, Inc.

58 Jumping Spider; 62 Assassin Bug with Prey/Stephen Dalton/Photo Researchers, Inc.

59 Ogre-faced Spider/Peter Chew

61 Honey-pot Ants/Mitsuaki Iwago/Minden Pictures

70 Caddis Fly Larva/Barbara Strnadova/Photo Researchers, Inc.

Color Insert

Housefly/Ron West/Educational Images Ltd., Elmira, NY. All rights reserved. Used by permission.

Ant and Aphids; Butterfly Metamorphosis (Steps 1, 3-6)/Mark Warner/Educational Images Ltd., Elmira, NY. All rights reserved. Used by permission.

Stalk-eyed Fly/Chin Fah Shin

Flowers/Laura Miller

Tarantula/Tom McHugh/Photo Researchers, Inc.

Diving Beetle/Jason Smalley

Australian Bulldog Ant/Michael Cermak

Bombardier Beetle/Thomas Eisner, Daniel Aneshansley, Cornell University

Puss Moth Caterpillar/David Glynne Fox

Bloody-nosed Beetle/Gary Bradley/ www.uksafari.com

Walking Stick Bug; Leaf Insect/Copyright © 2002 Ripley Entertainment Inc. and its licensors. All rights reserved.

Peacock Katydid; Treehopper/Dr. James L. Castner

Orchid Mantis/Justin Peach/Image Quest 3-D

Swallowtail Butterfly Larva/John Alcock

Butterfly Metamorphosis (Step 2)/Educational Images Ltd., Elmira, NY. All rights reserved. Used by permission.

Tsetse Fly/Peter Parks/Image Quest 3-D

Parasitic Wasp Cocoons on Caterpillar/Clemson University Department of Entomology, Cooperative Extension Service

Cover

Puss Moth Caterpillar/David Glynne Fox

Peacock Katydid; Wax-tailed Planthopper; Spiny Caterpillar/Dr. James L. Castner

Don't miss these other exciting

books . . .

**World's
Weirdest
Critters**

Creepy Stuff

**Odd-inary
People**

**Amazing
Escapes**

If you enjoyed **Bizarre Bugs**, get ready for

 **World's Weirdest Gadgets**

You'll be amazed at the marvels of ingenuity inventors have dreamed up—or discovered quite by accident . . .

Martin Goetze invented
a device for making dimples in 1896

At age six, Susan Goodin invented the
Edible Cat Spoon, a handy garlic-flavored spoon
that could go right in the dish with the cat food

Percy Spencer accidentally discovered the key to
microwave cooking when a nearby tube used in
radar sets melted a candy bar in his pocket

In 1883, Jack Ferry crossed the English
Channel on his giant tricycle

There are a lot of clever inventors out there—and just as many wacky inventions. Read all about them in **World's Weirdest Gadgets!**